AF269729

Spotlight on
Tap Dancing

Hannah Gramson

Lerner Publications ◆ Minneapolis

Lerner Publications Company
An imprint of Lerner Publishing Group, Inc.
241 First Avenue North
Minneapolis, MN 55401 USA

For reading levels and more information, look up this title at www.lernerbooks.com.

Main body text set in Mikado.
Typeface provided by HVD.

Editor: Annie Zheng **Designer:** Mary Ross

Library of Congress Cataloging-in-Publication Data

Names: Gramson, Hannah, author.
Title: Spotlight on tap dancing / Hannah Gramson.
Description: Minneapolis, MN : Lerner Publications Company, [2024] | Series: Lerner sports rookie. Just dance | Includes bibliographical references and index. | Audience: Ages 5–8 years | Audience: Grades 2–3 | Summary: "Tap is all about finding your feet! Readers will pick up slick tips on what to wear, how to step, and making noise in this fun, upbeat dance style"– Provided by publisher.
Identifiers: LCCN 2023043742 (print) | LCCN 2023043743 (ebook) | ISBN 9798765625699 (lib. bdg.) | ISBN 9798765628874 (pbk.) | ISBN 9798765634165 (epub)
Subjects: LCSH: Tap dancing–Juvenile literature. | Jazz tap–Juvenile literature. | Tap dancers–Juvenile literature. | Tap dance music–Juvenile literature.
 Classification: LCC GV1794 .G69 2024 (print) | LCC GV1794 (ebook) | DDC 792.7/8–dc23/eng/20230925

LC record available at https://lccn.loc.gov/2023043742
LC ebook record available at https://lccn.loc.gov/2023043743

Manufactured in the United States of America
1-1010142-51903-2/5/2024

Table of Contents

Chapter 1 Welcome to Tap   4

Chapter 2 Tap It Out   10

Chapter 3 Find Your Feet   14

Chapter 4 Tap Up a Storm!   20

Glossary   24

Learn More   24

Index   24

Chapter 1
Welcome to Tap

Tap! Smack! Stomp! The dancer makes a lot of noise as they move across the floor. They're doing a tap dance!

Tap started in the United States. People created it by mixing dance styles from Africa and Europe.

> ★ **Fun Fact** ★
>
> **May 25 is National Tap Dance Day!**

7

The two main types of tap dance are rhythm and Broadway.

You can see tap performed in many musicals.

Tap It Out

Tap dancers wear shoes with metal plates on the heels and toes.

They make clicking sounds
when they hit hard surfaces.

Dancers can make different sounds by moving their feet in different ways.

★ **Fun Fact** ★

Early tap shoes had pennies or nails hammered onto the bottoms.

Find Your Feet

Tap is fast-paced. You'll learn to do the steps slowly at first. Then you'll get faster over time.

★ Tip ★
Focus on your
movement!

One of the first steps you'll learn is a brush. A brush is when you move your foot forward or backward.

★ Tip ★

Relax your ankles! This helps make your steps look clean.

As you do, you hit the floor
with just the ball of your foot.

There are a lot
of different
tap steps.
Dancers put
them together
in combinations.

★ Up Close! ★

How to Do the Maxi Ford

- Jump onto your right foot.
- Brush your left foot forward, then backward.
- Jump onto your left foot.
- Tap your right toe behind your left foot.

Tap Up a Storm!

You can tap dance alone, with a partner, or in a group. You can tap dance just for fun. Or you can perform on a stage.

Some people tap dance in musicals.
Others perform in recitals.

Tap is an upbeat style of dance.
So have fun and make some noise!

23

Glossary

ball: the rounded part of the human foot that is at the bottom of the foot and below the toes

combination: combining two or more dance steps

upbeat: cheerful

Learn More

Castrovilla, Selene. *This Is Tap: Savion Glover Finds His Funk*. New York: Holiday House, 2023.

Hammond, Mel. *Spotlight on Stepping*. Minneapolis: Lerner Publications, 2025.

Murray, Julie. *Competitive Dance*. Minneapolis: Abdo Kids, 2023.

Index

Broadway, 8
brush, 16, 19

Maxi Ford, 19

rhythm, 8

Photo Acknowledgments

Image credits: ti-ja/Getty Images, p. 5; Jack Vartoogian/Getty Images, p. 7; Featureflash Photo Agency/Shutterstock, p. 9; kbycphotography/Getty Images, p. 11; Krysja/Shutterstock, p. 13; South China Morning Post/Getty Images, p. 15; Dmitri Kotchetov/Shutterstock, p. 17; adamkaz/Getty Images, p. 18; BearFotos/Shutterstock, p. 19; AP Photo/Yui Mokm, p. 21; George Shelley/Getty Images, p. 23.
Design elements: Kilroy79/Getty Images; Iuliia Mashinets/Getty Images.
Cover: adamkaz/Getty Images.